Lets Color Some Pottery

Color on original sketchbook ideas and designs for ceramic pottery by Janvier Miller. A coloring book for all ages.

by Janvier Miller

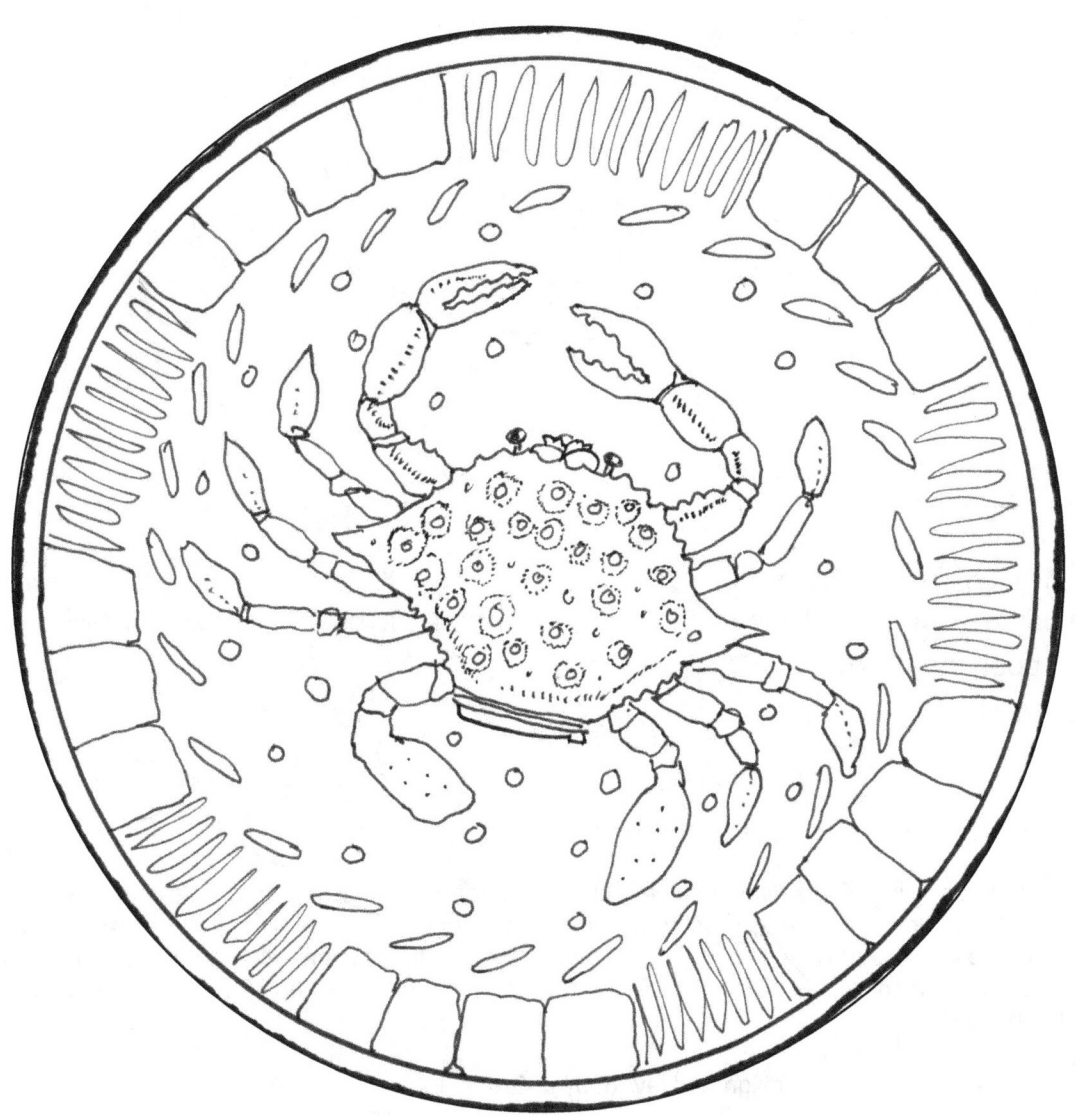

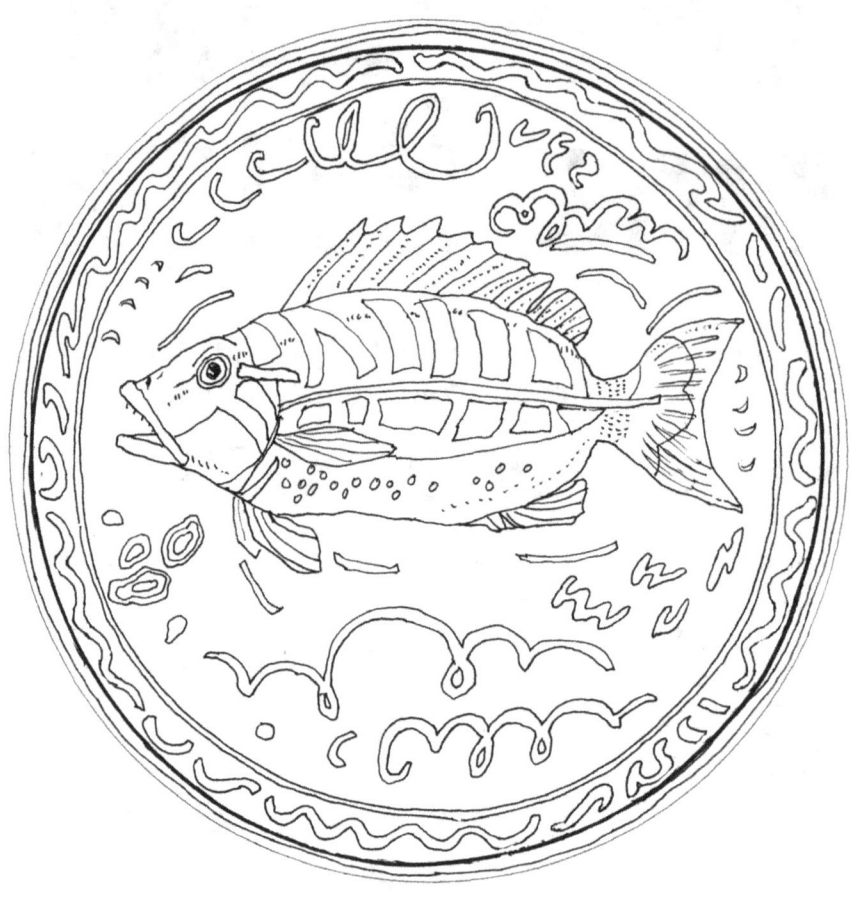

Lets Color Some Pottery

Color on original sketchbook ideas and designs for ceramic pottery by Janvier Miller.
A coloring book for all ages.

By Janvier Miller

Art consultant Gustaf Miller, Book design and layout by J. Bruce Jones

Janvier Miller
www.janvierpainter.blogspot.com/

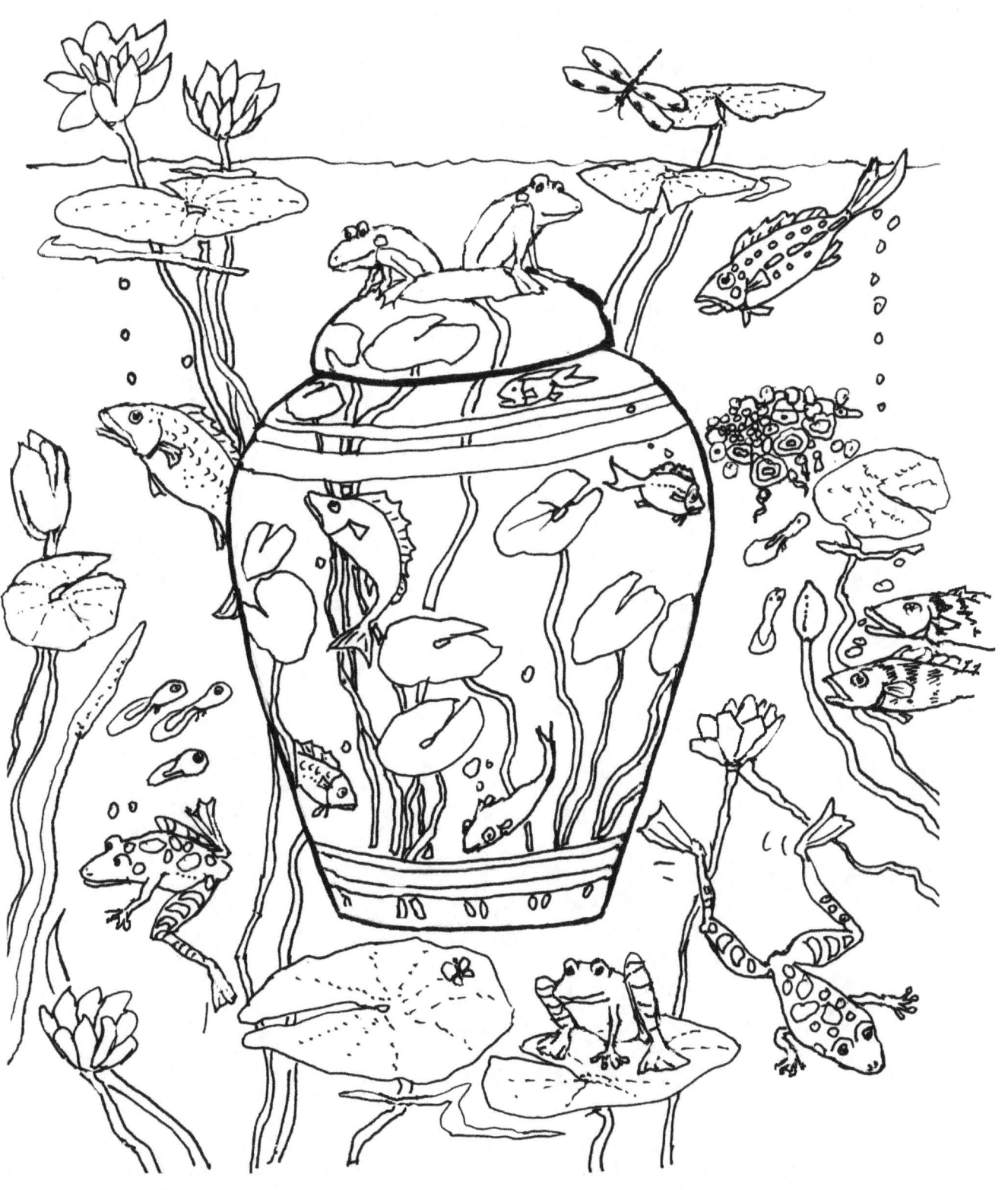

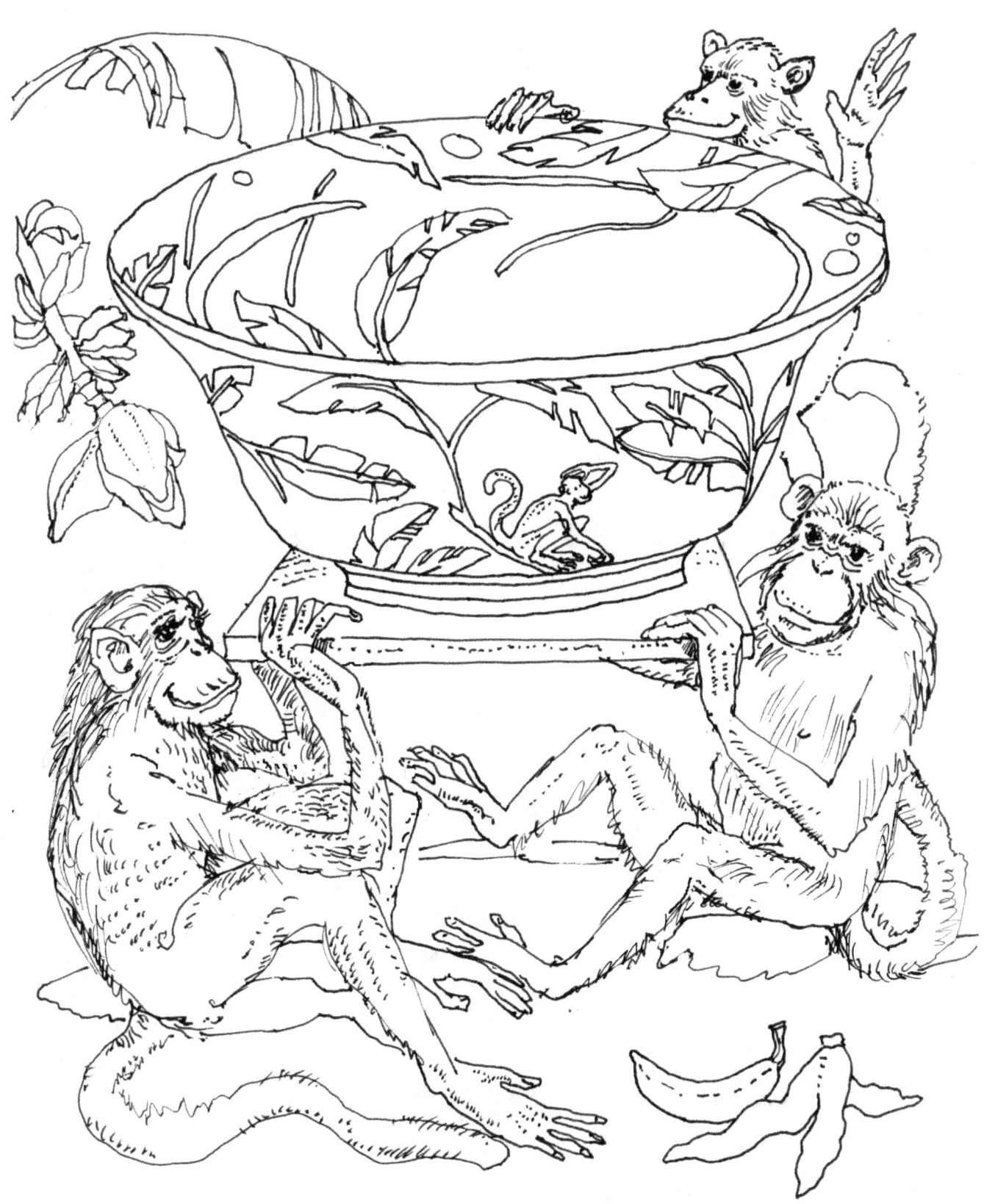

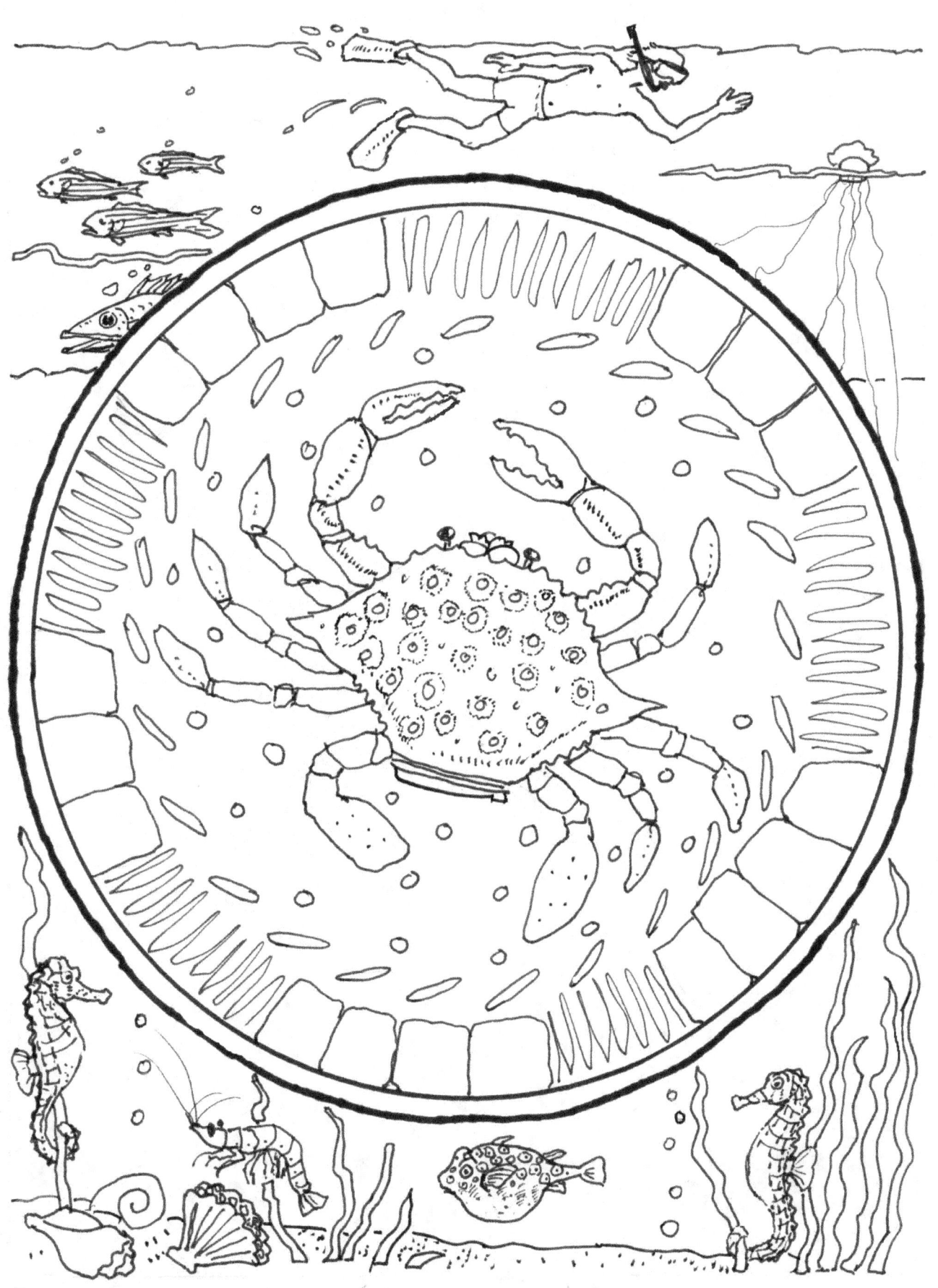

swim & snorkle

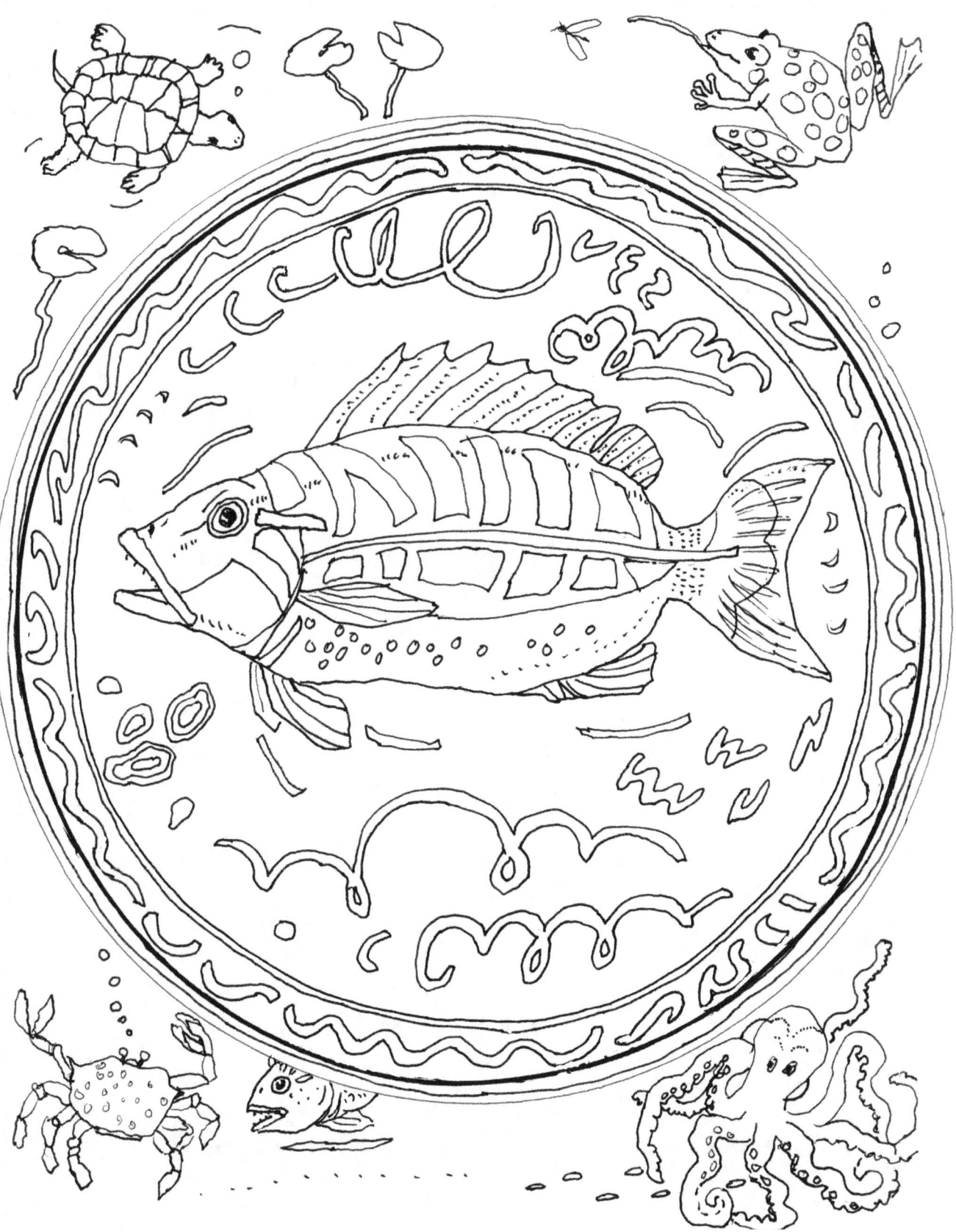

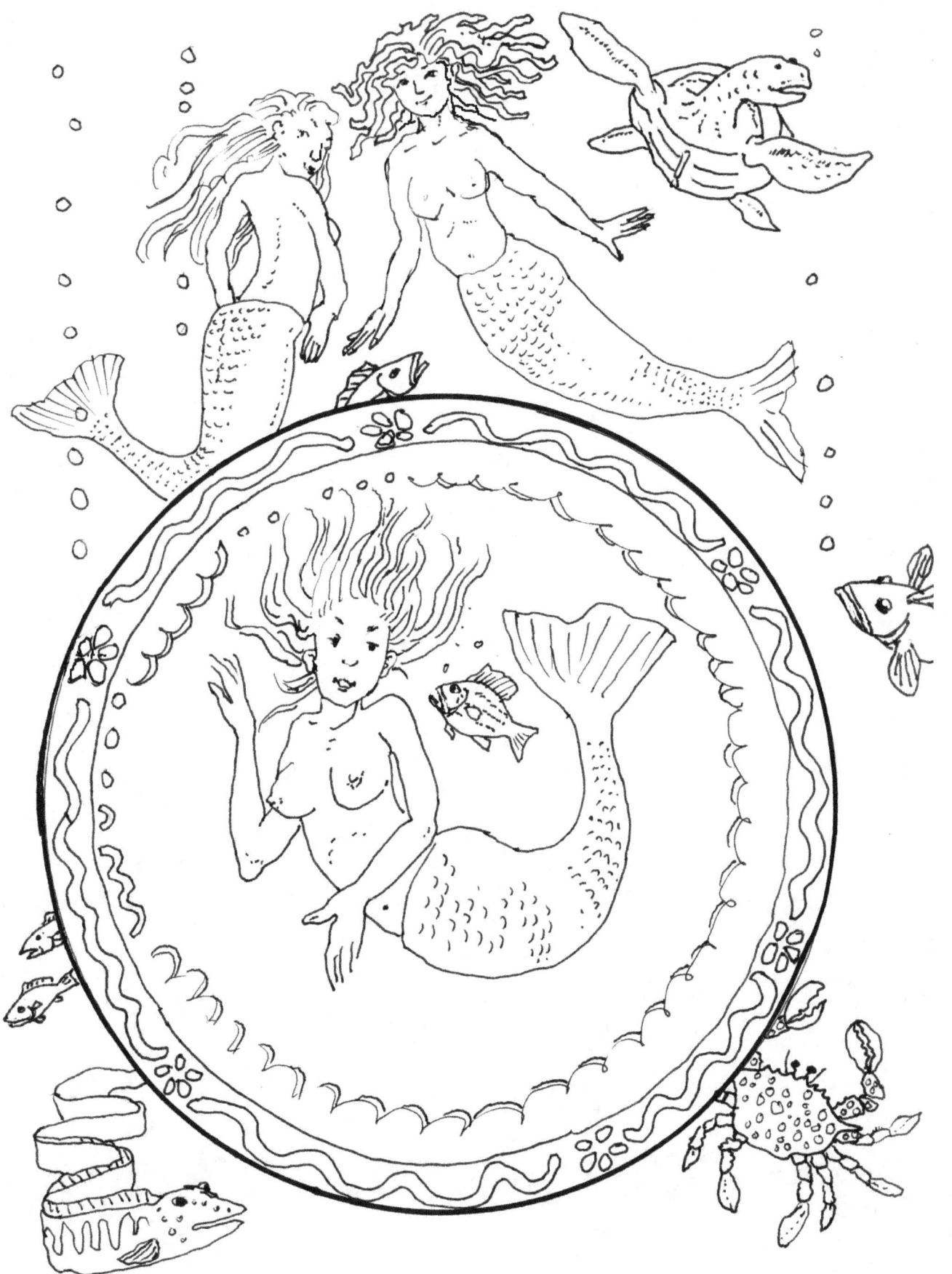

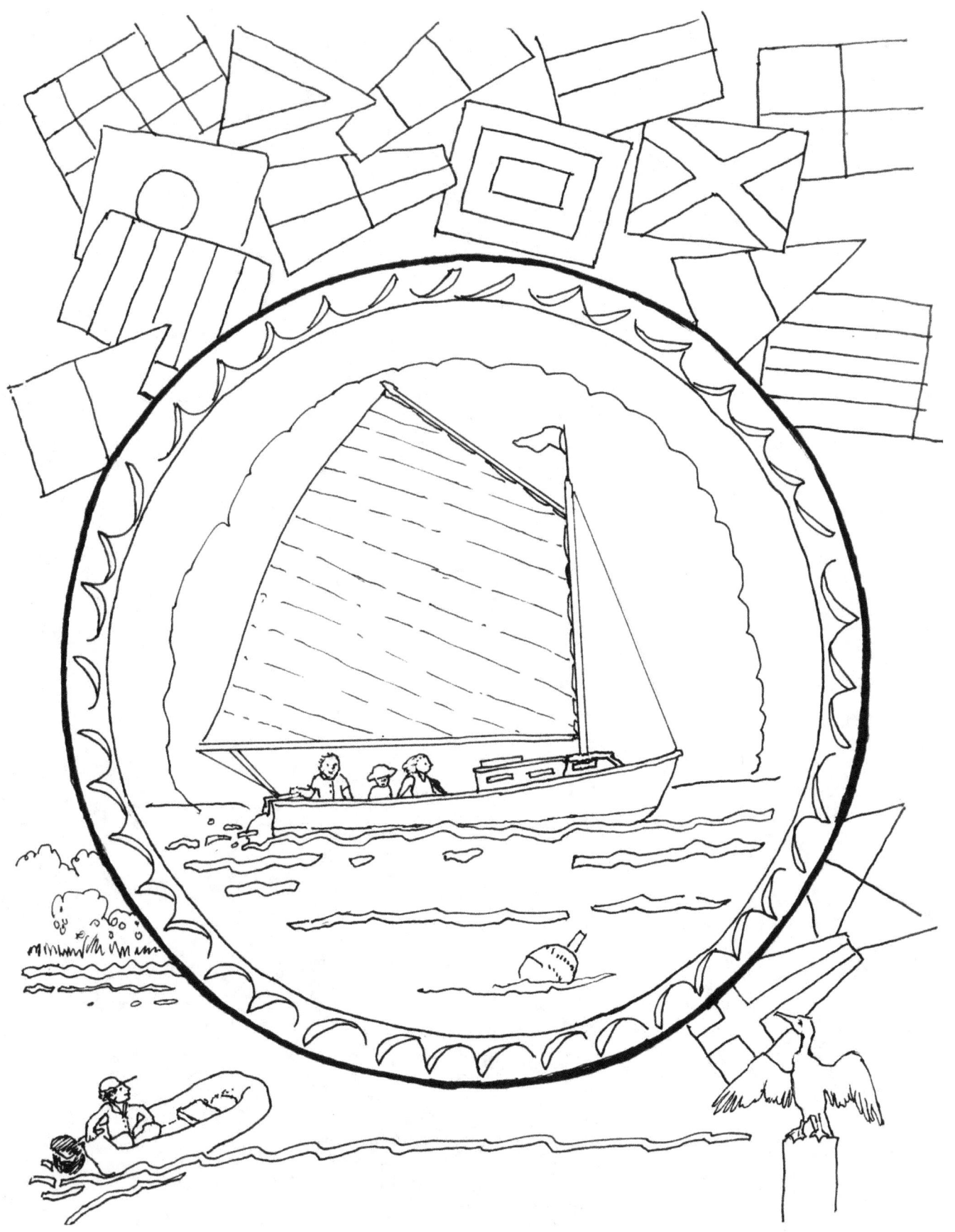

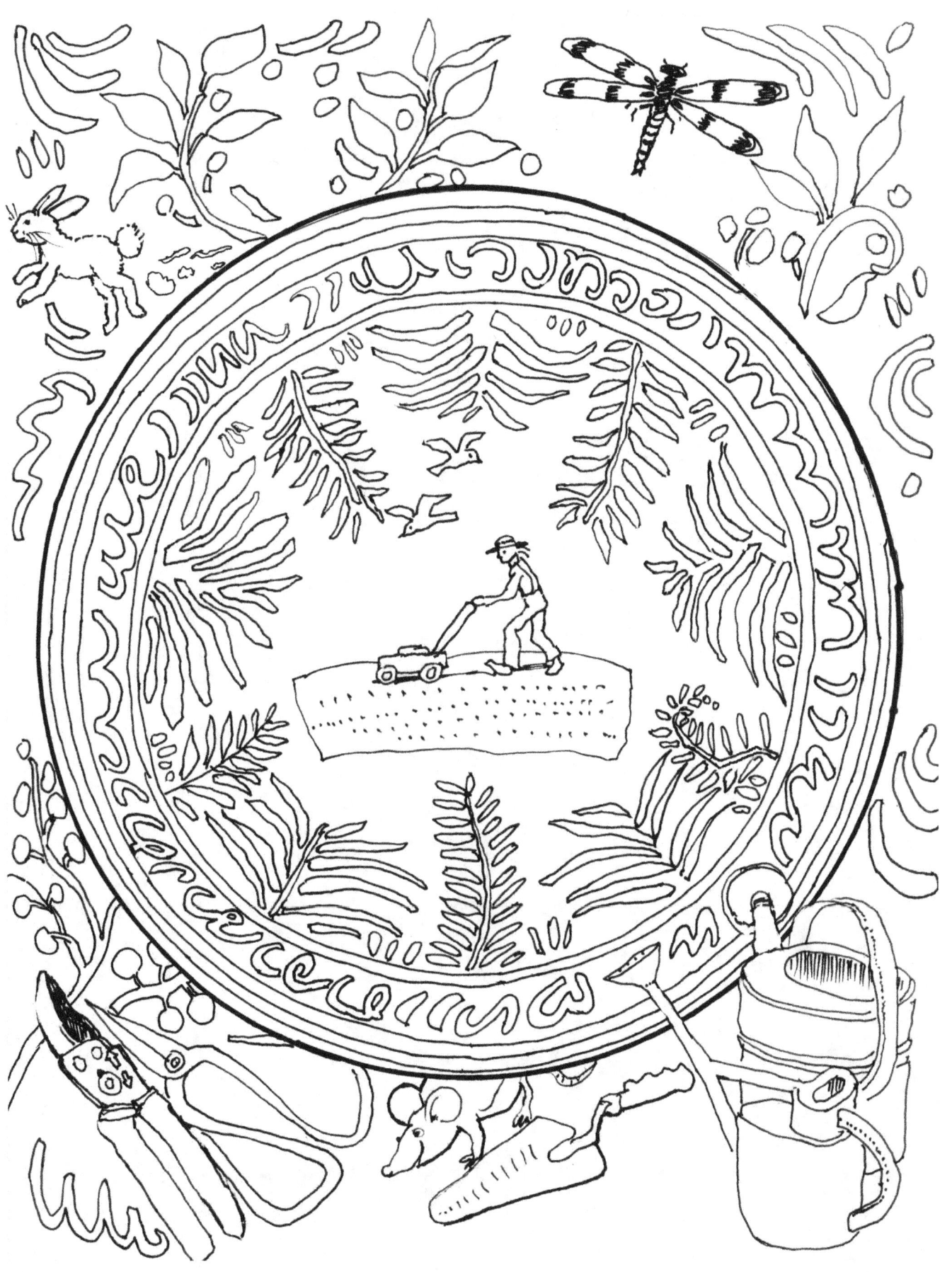

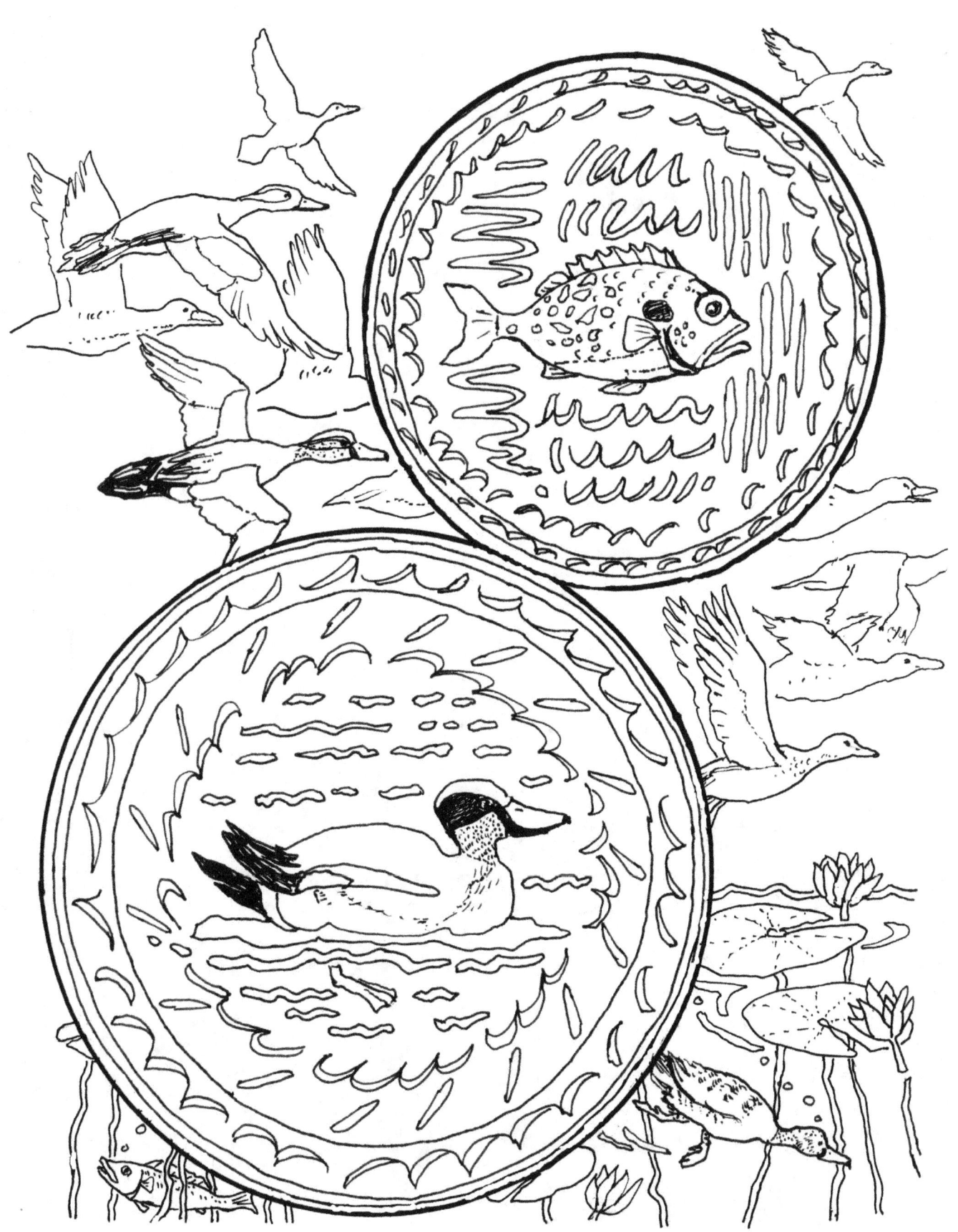

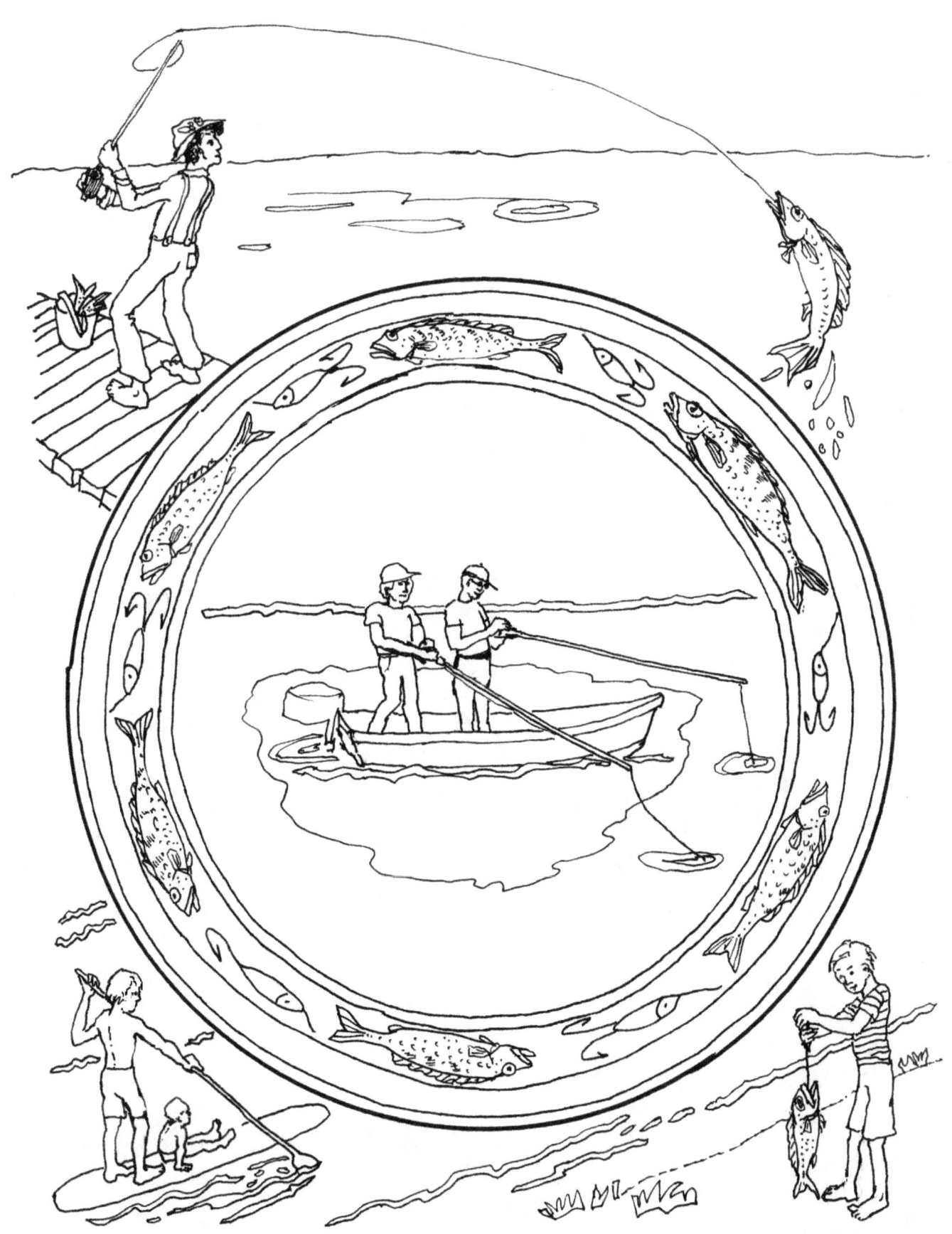

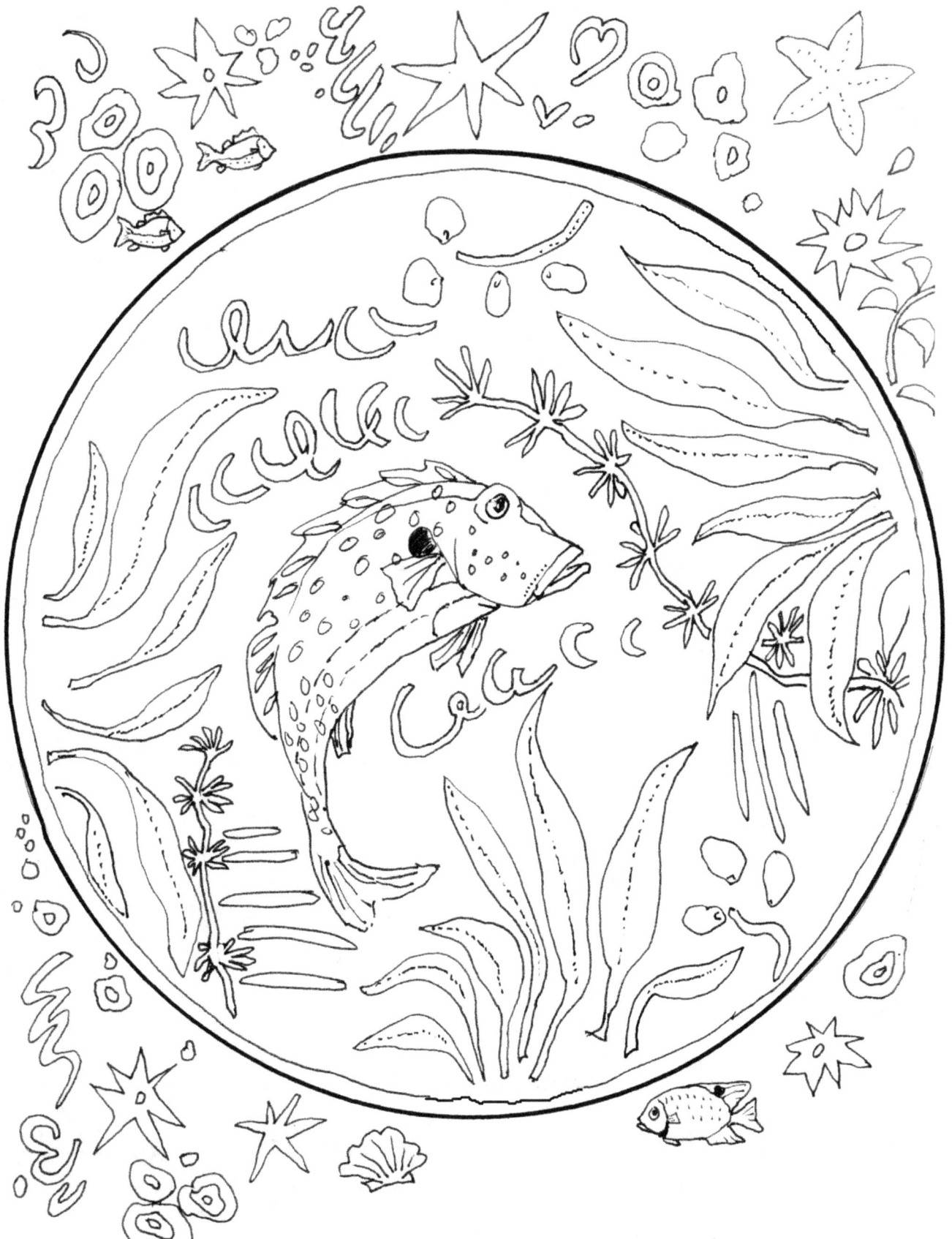

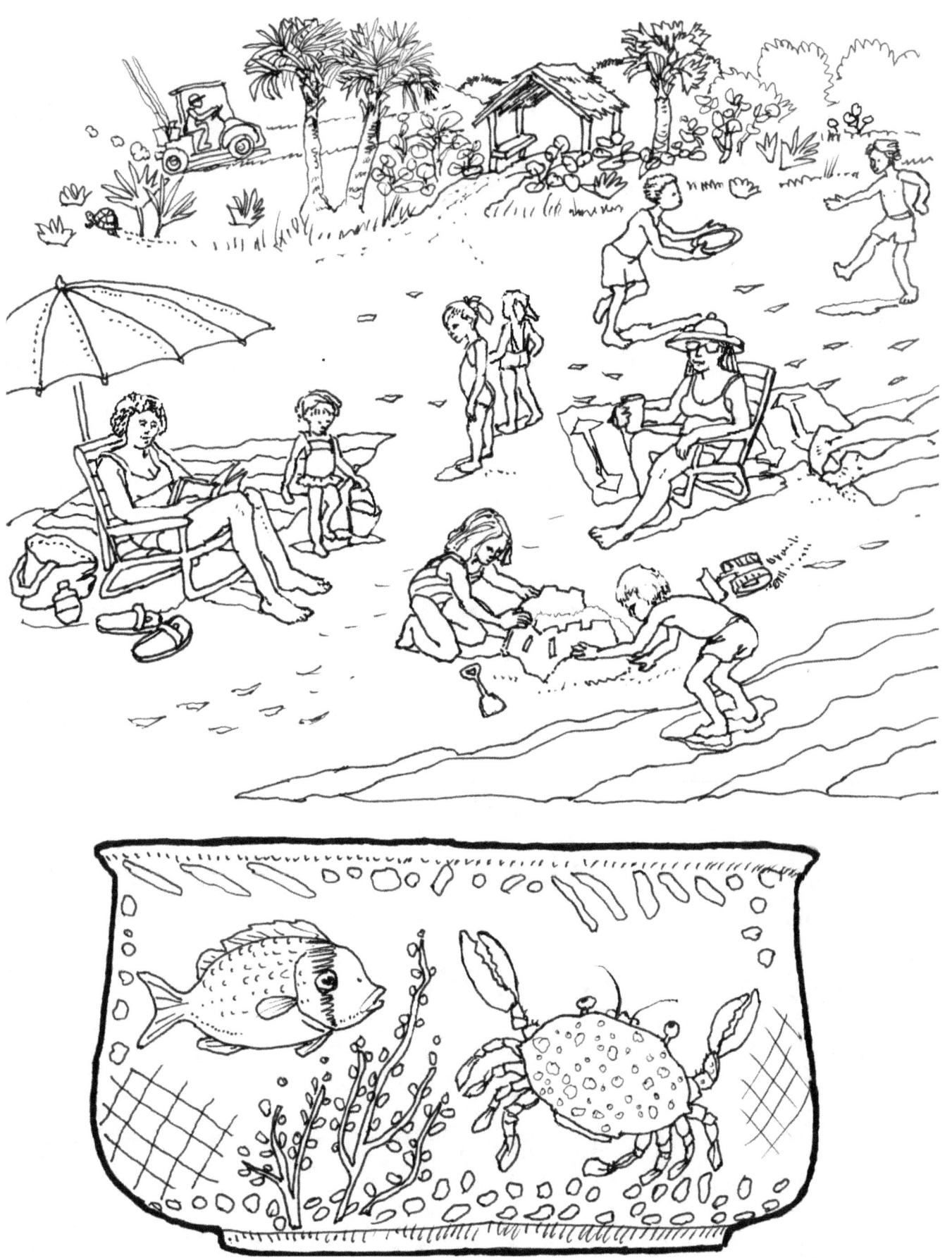

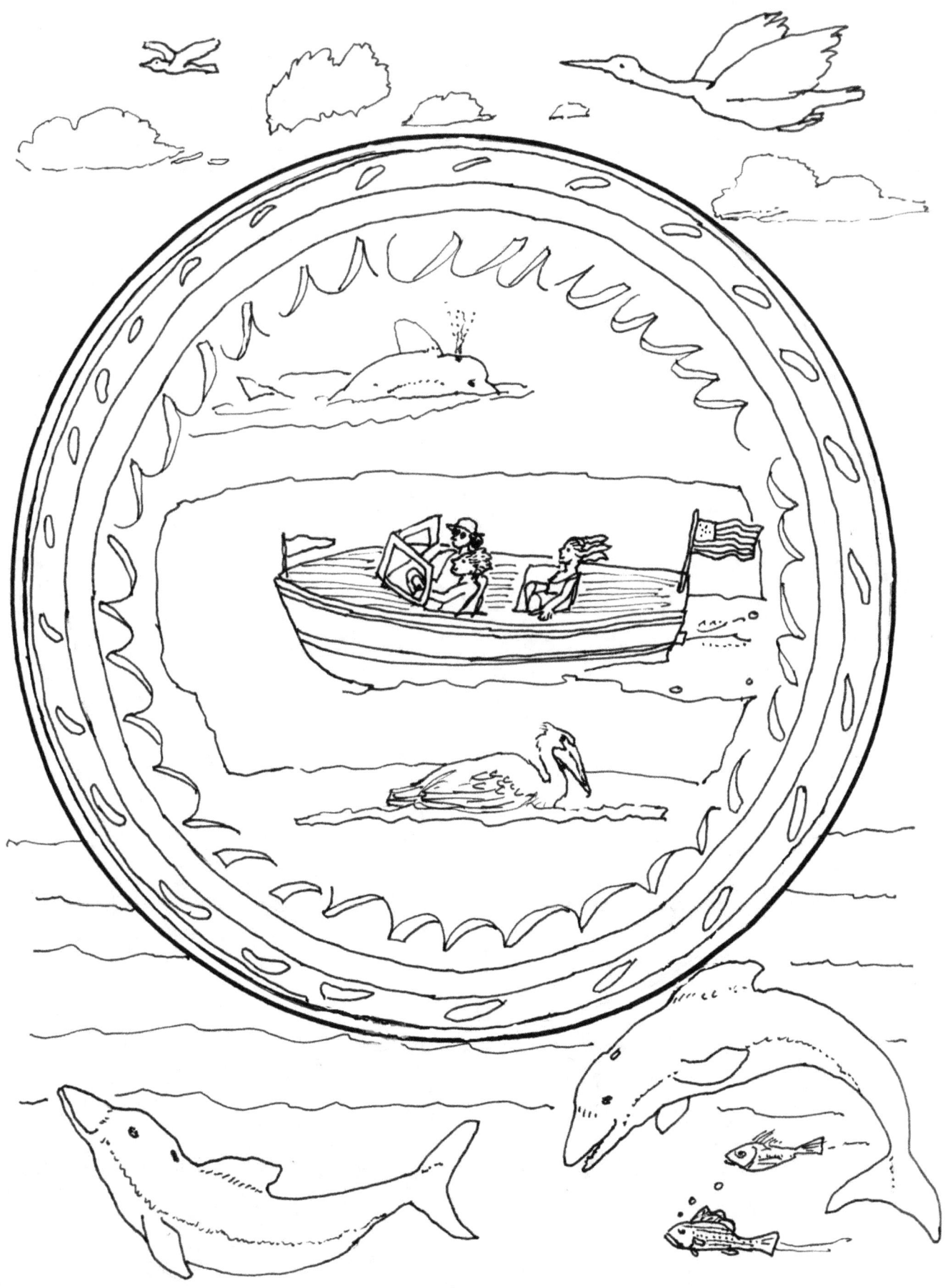

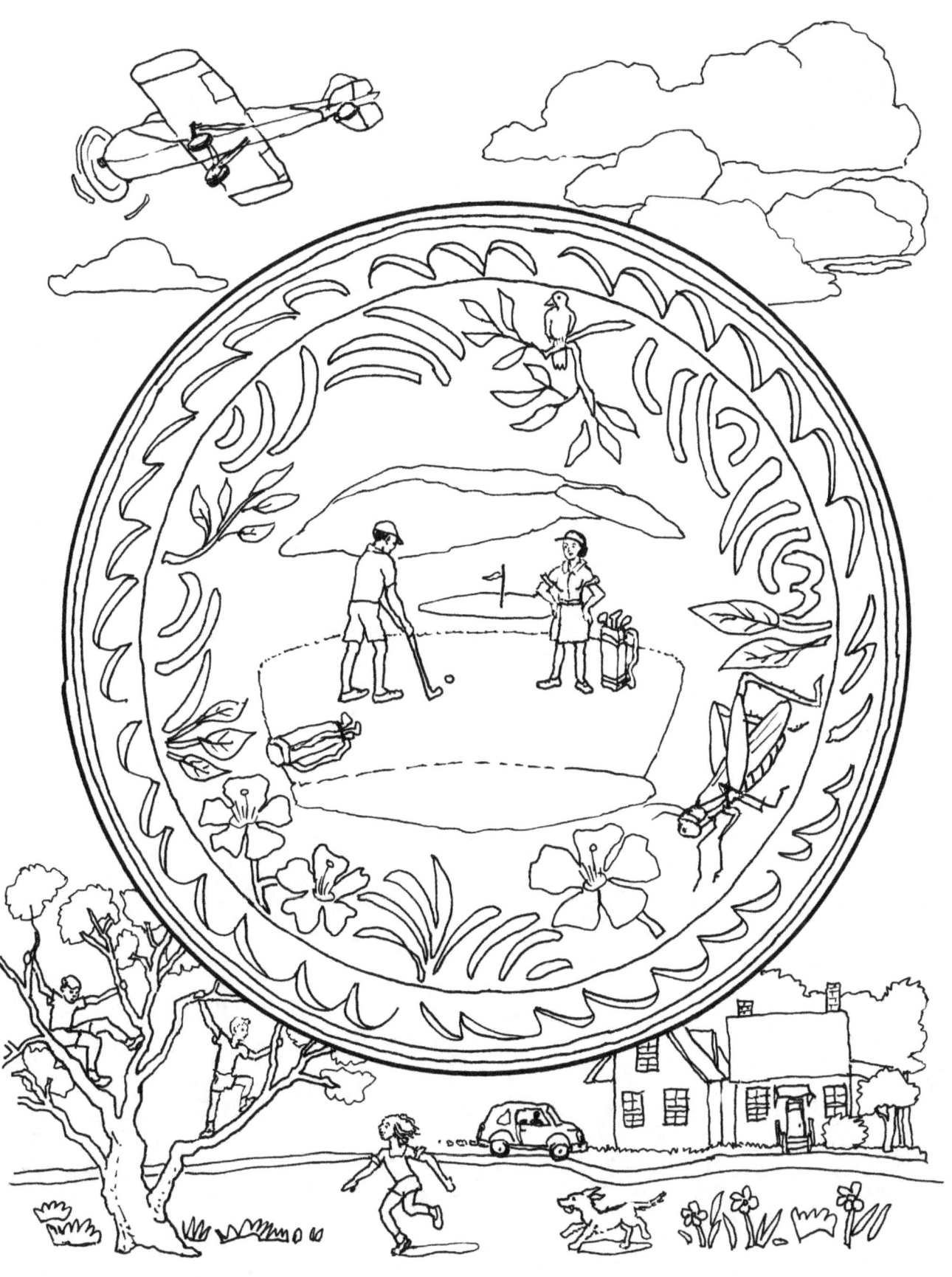

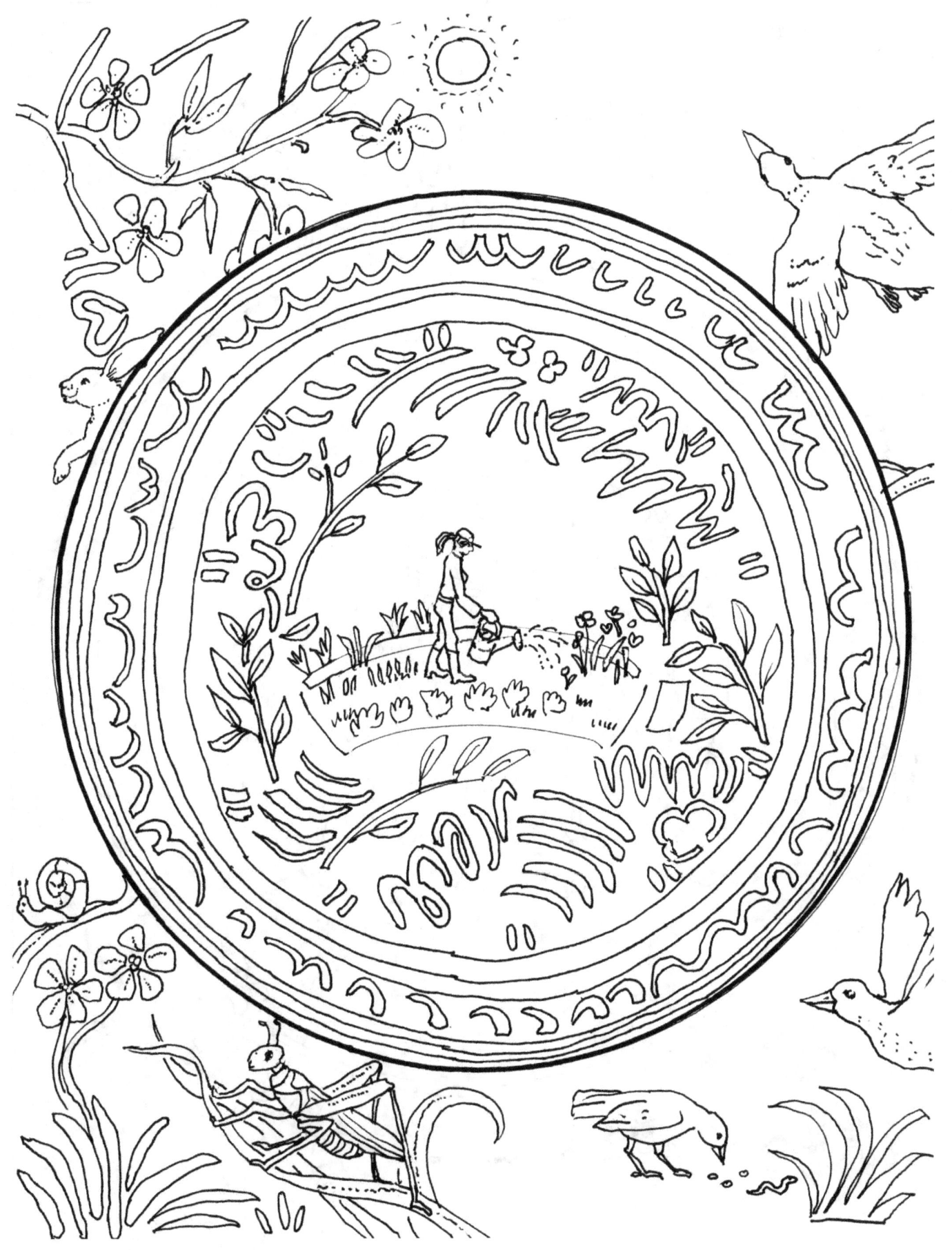

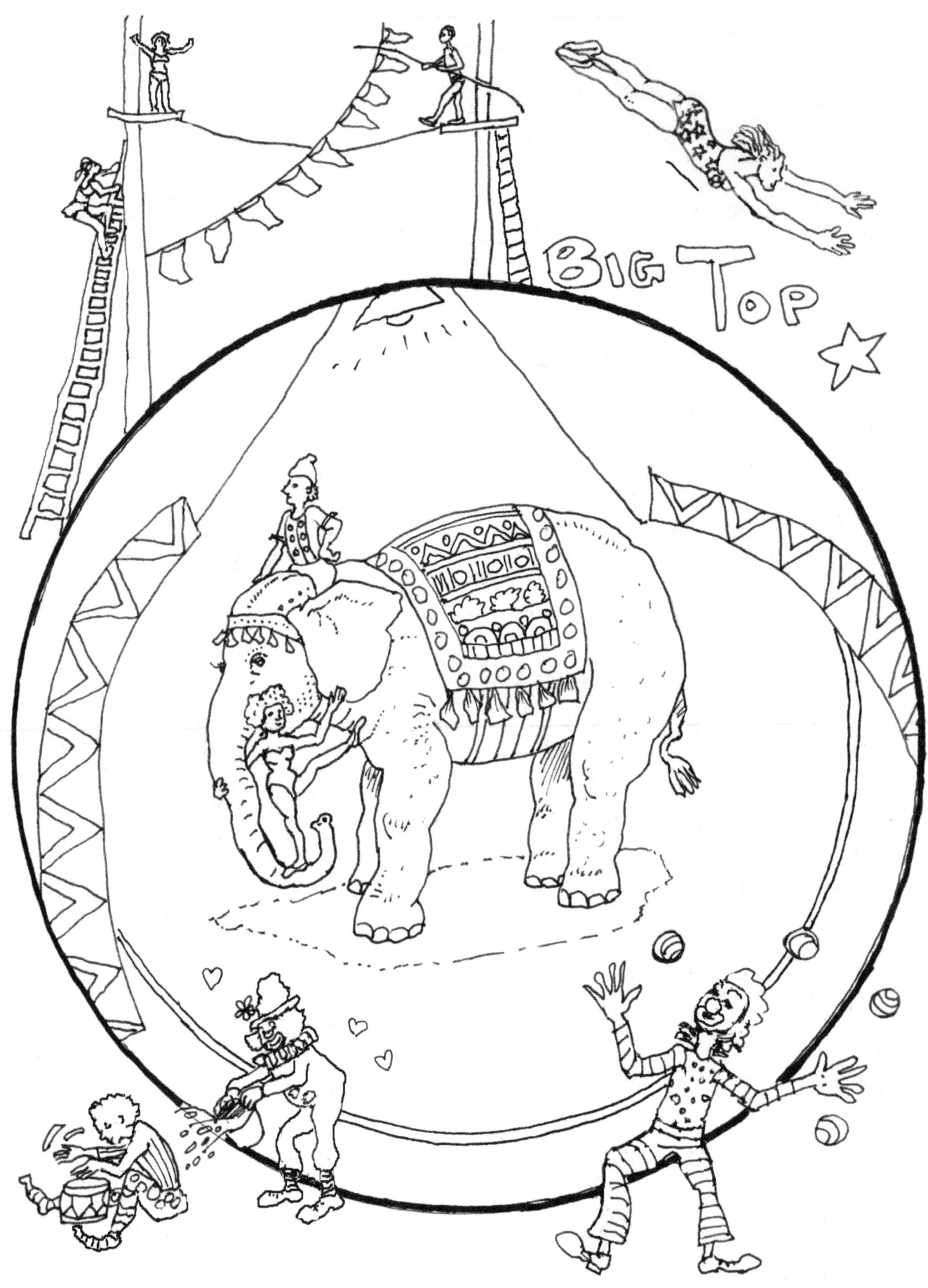

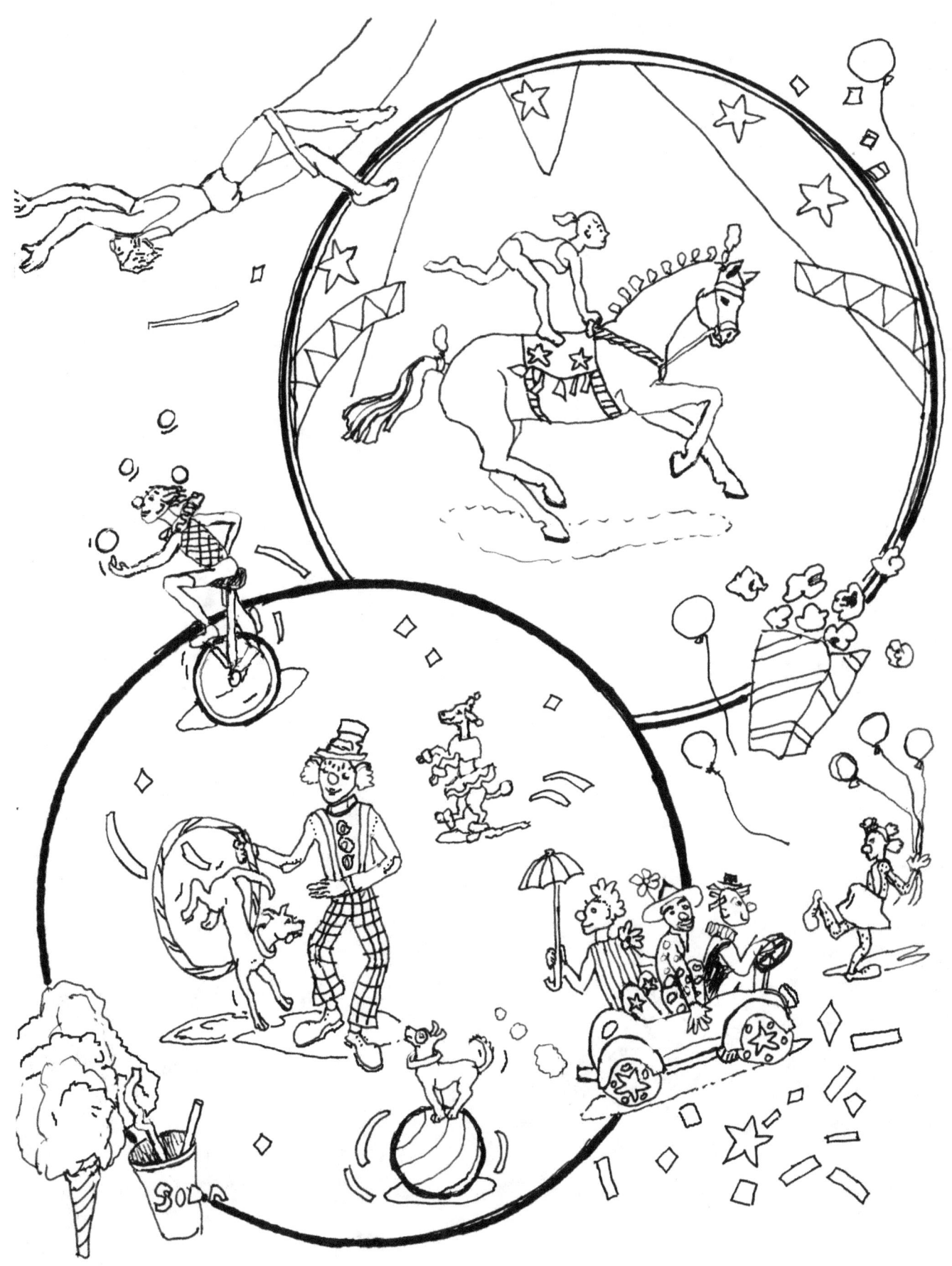

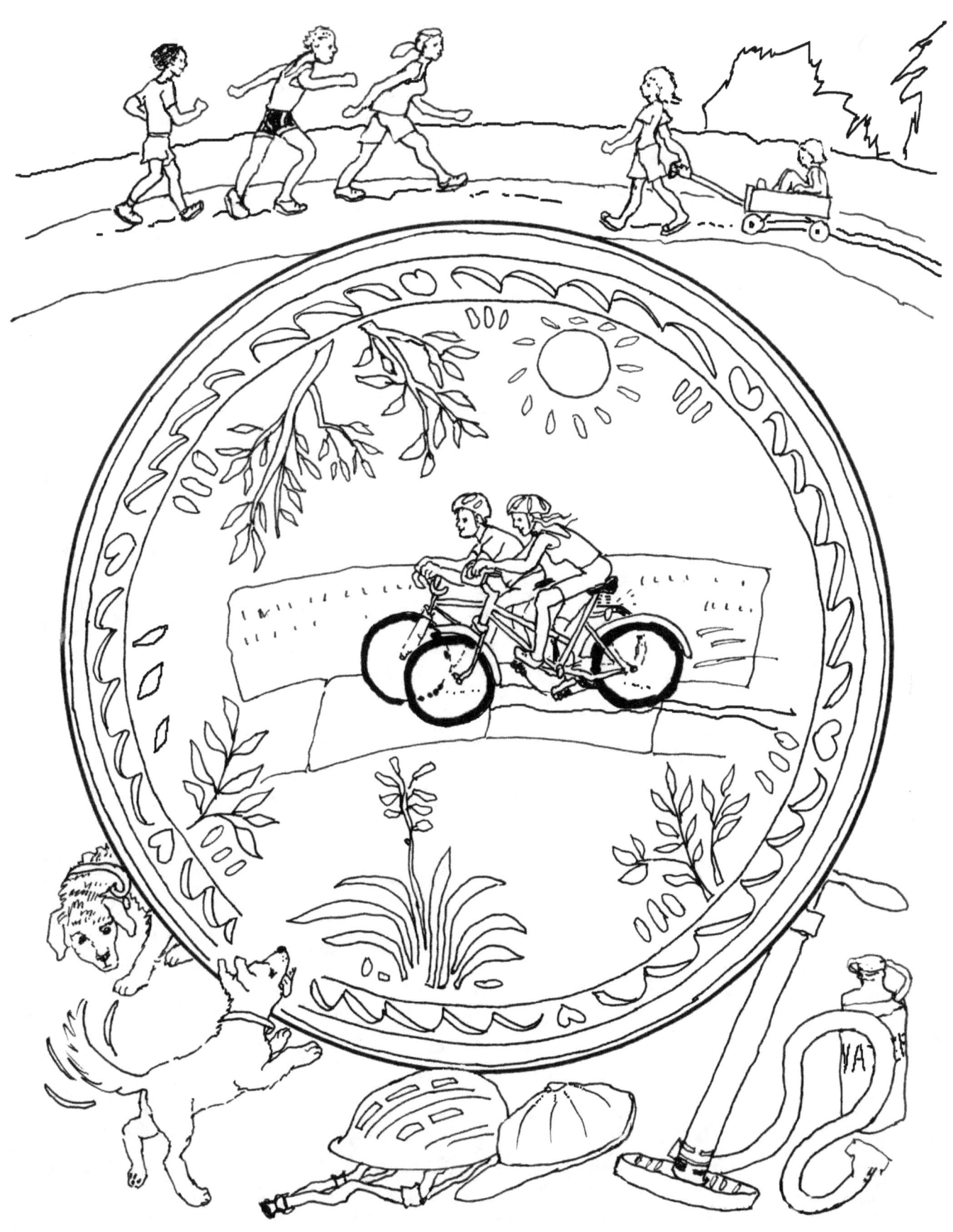

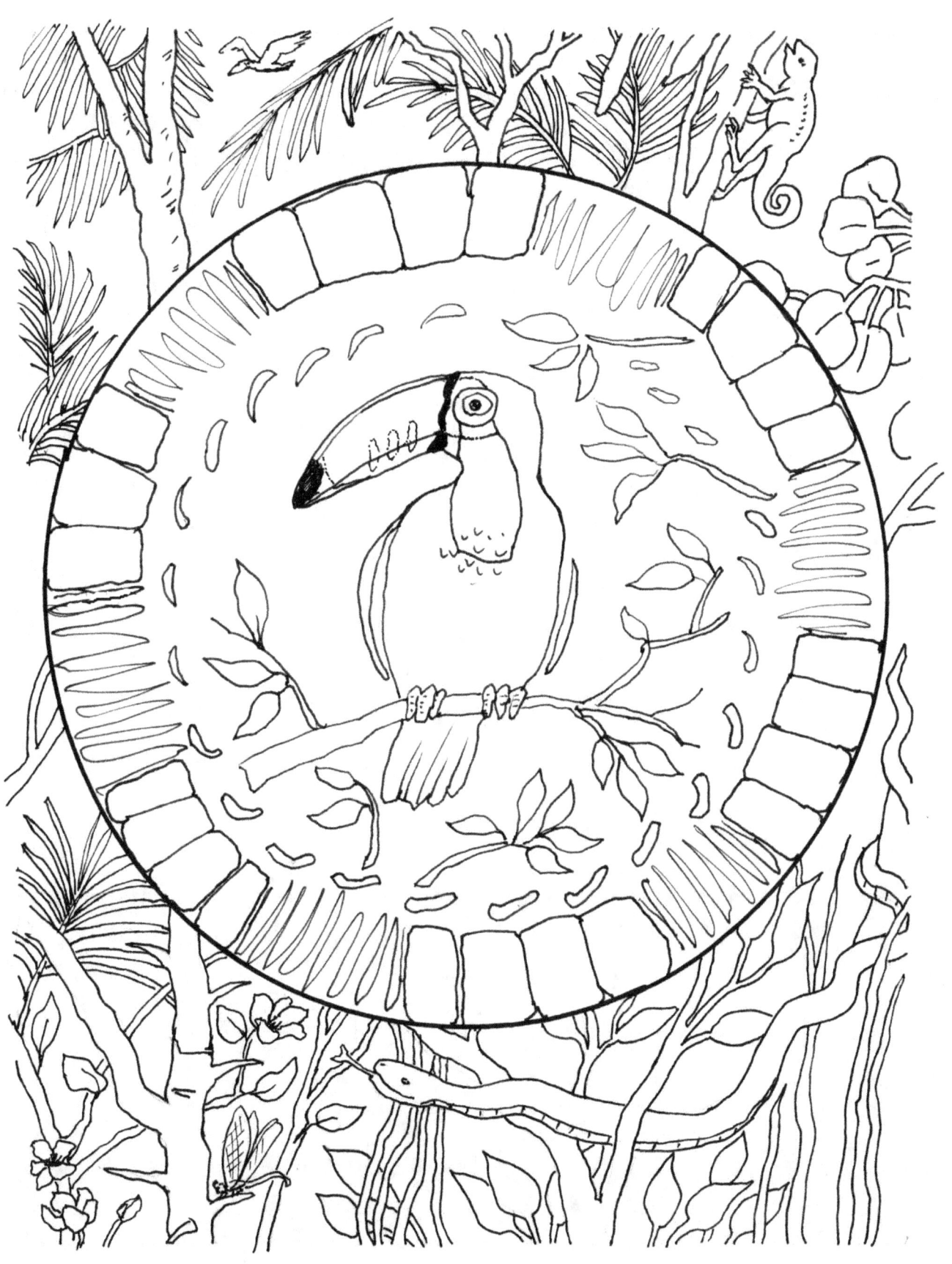

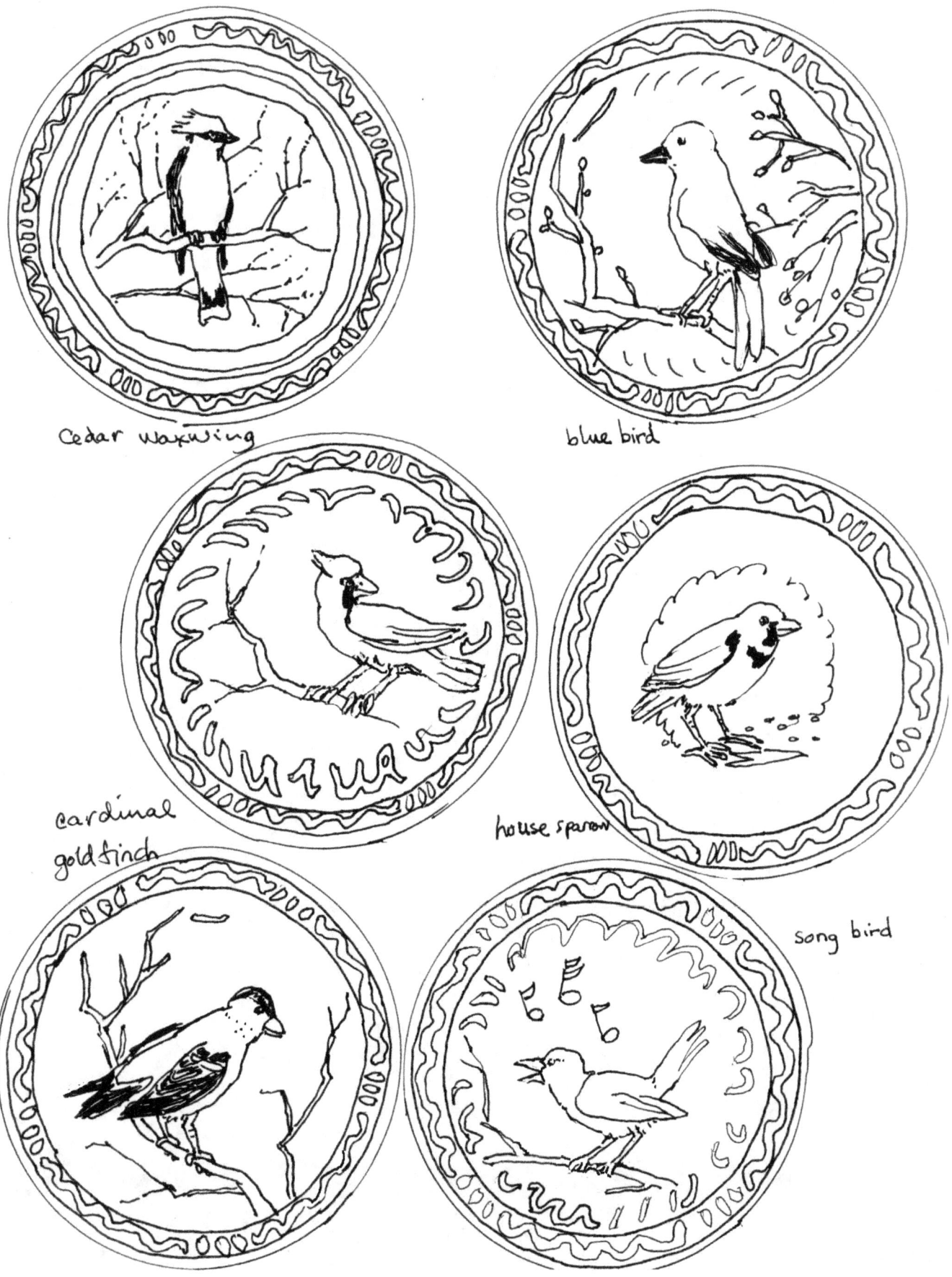

cedar waxwing

blue bird

cardinal
goldfinch

house sparrow

song bird

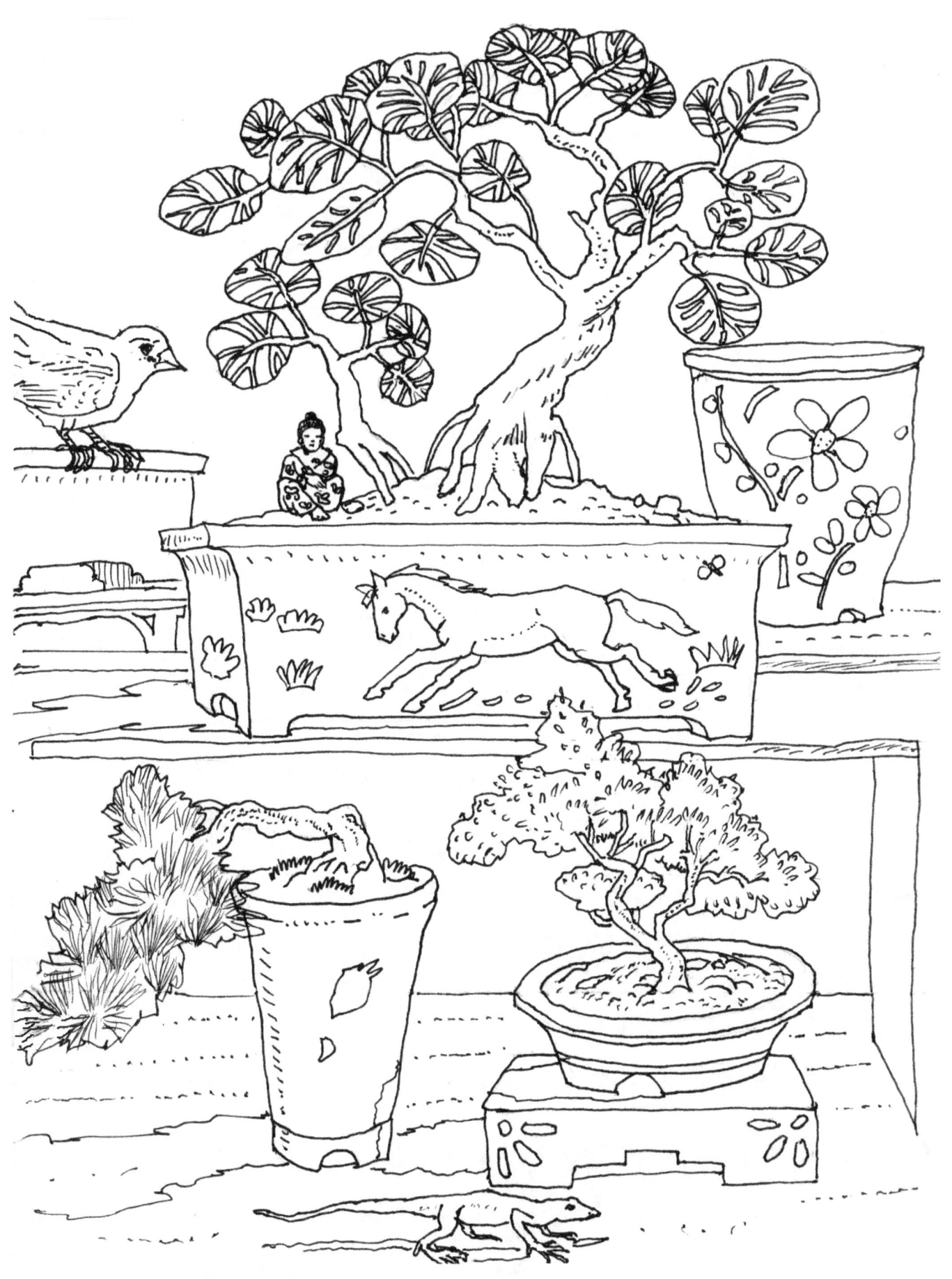

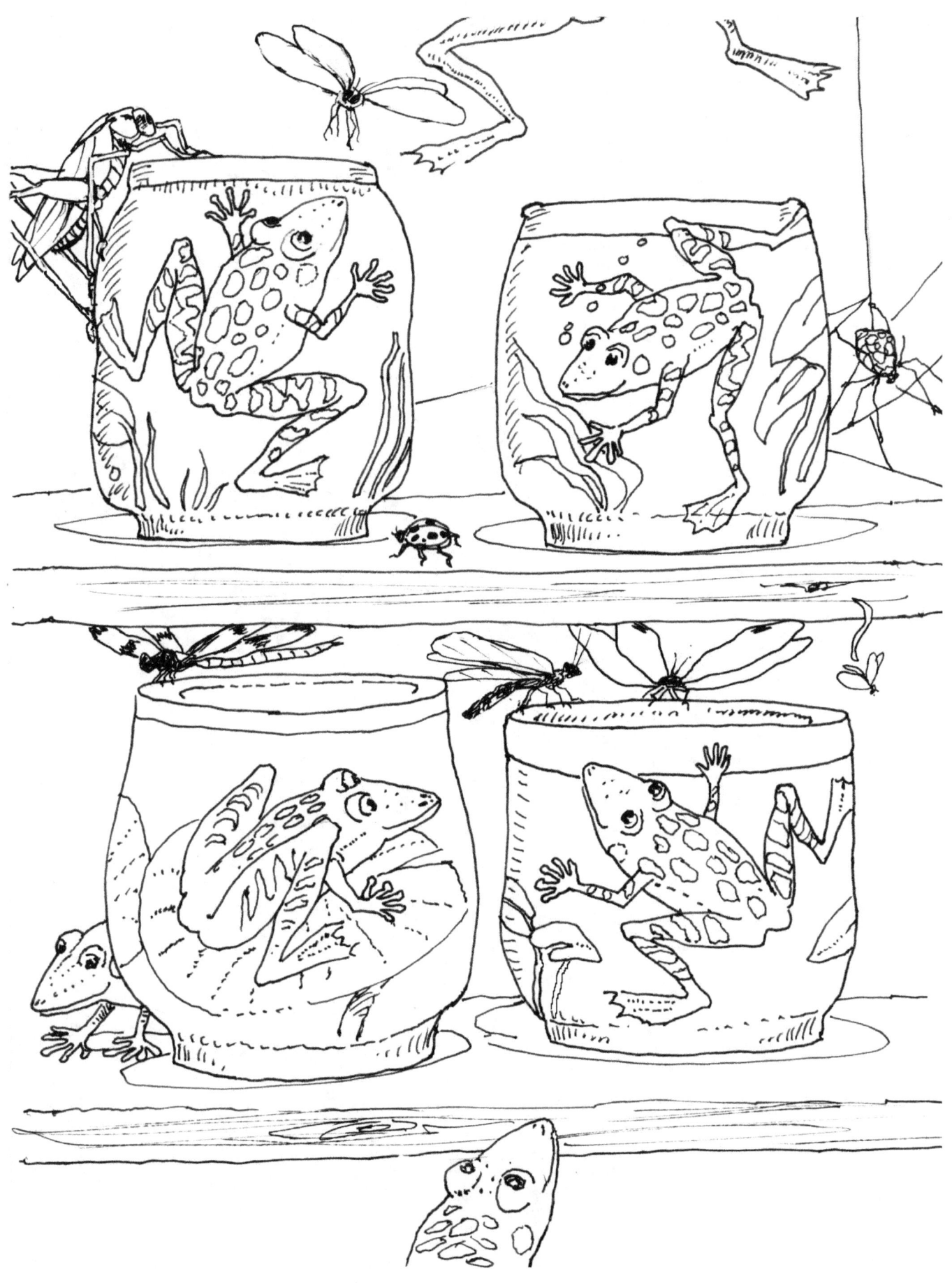

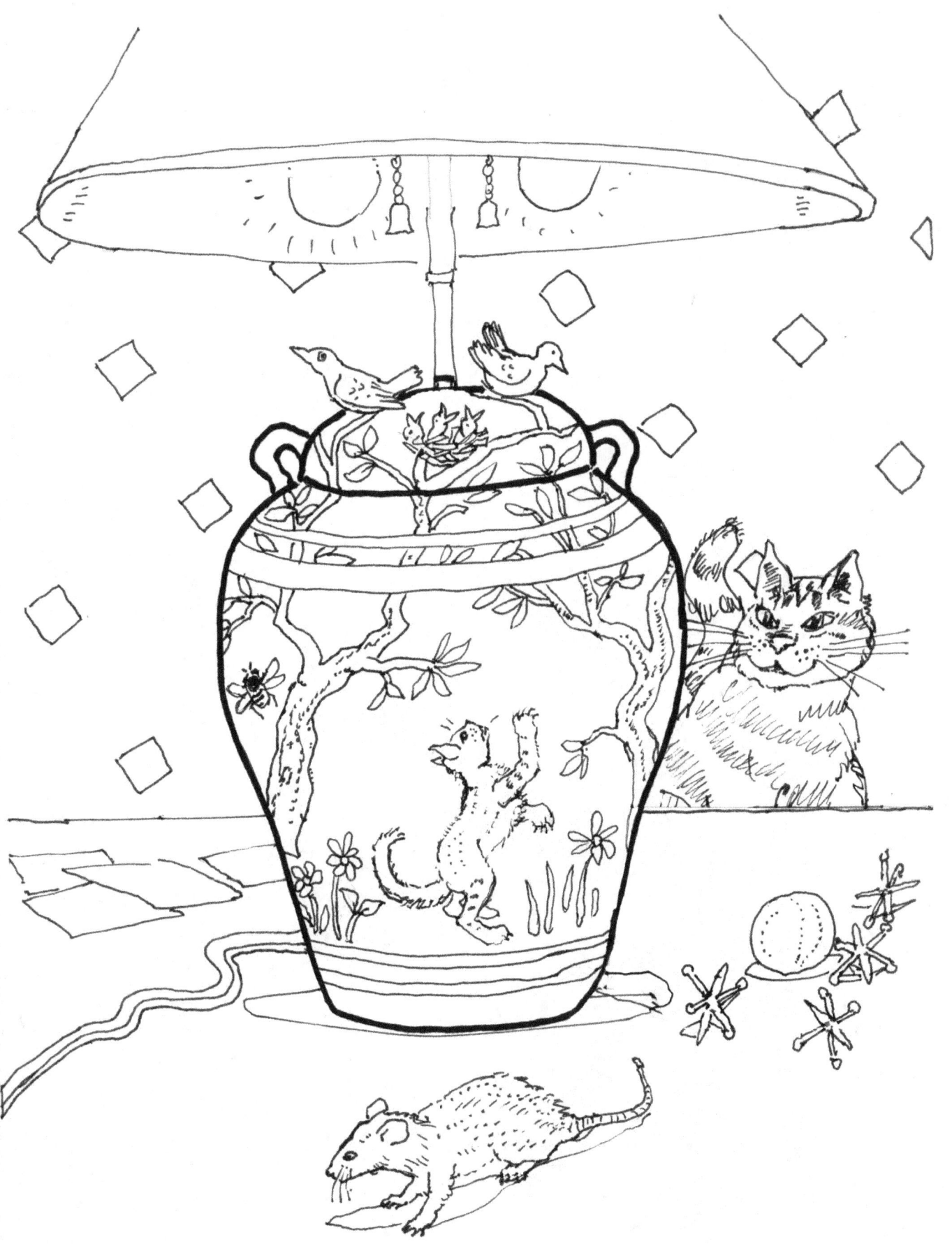

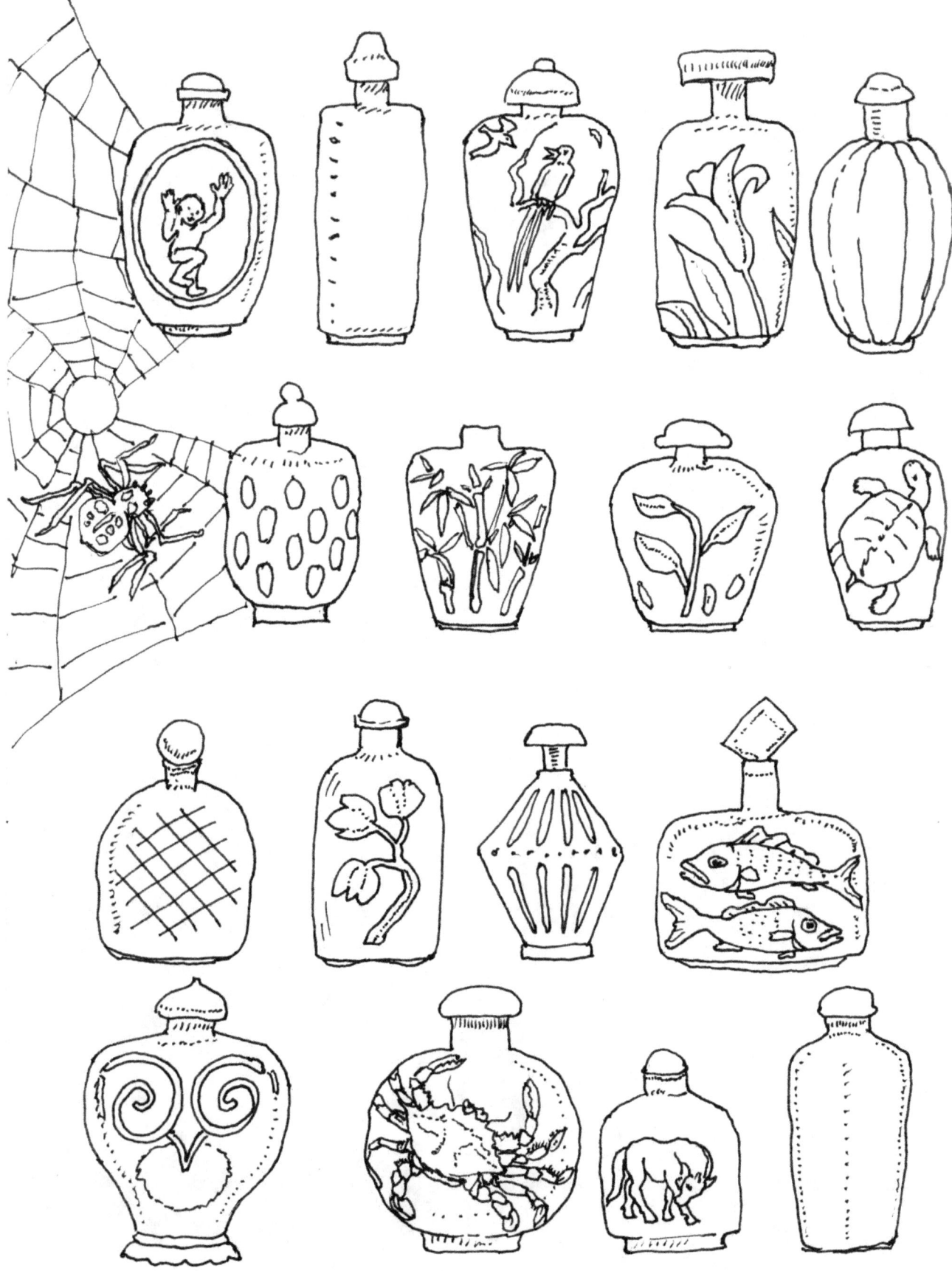

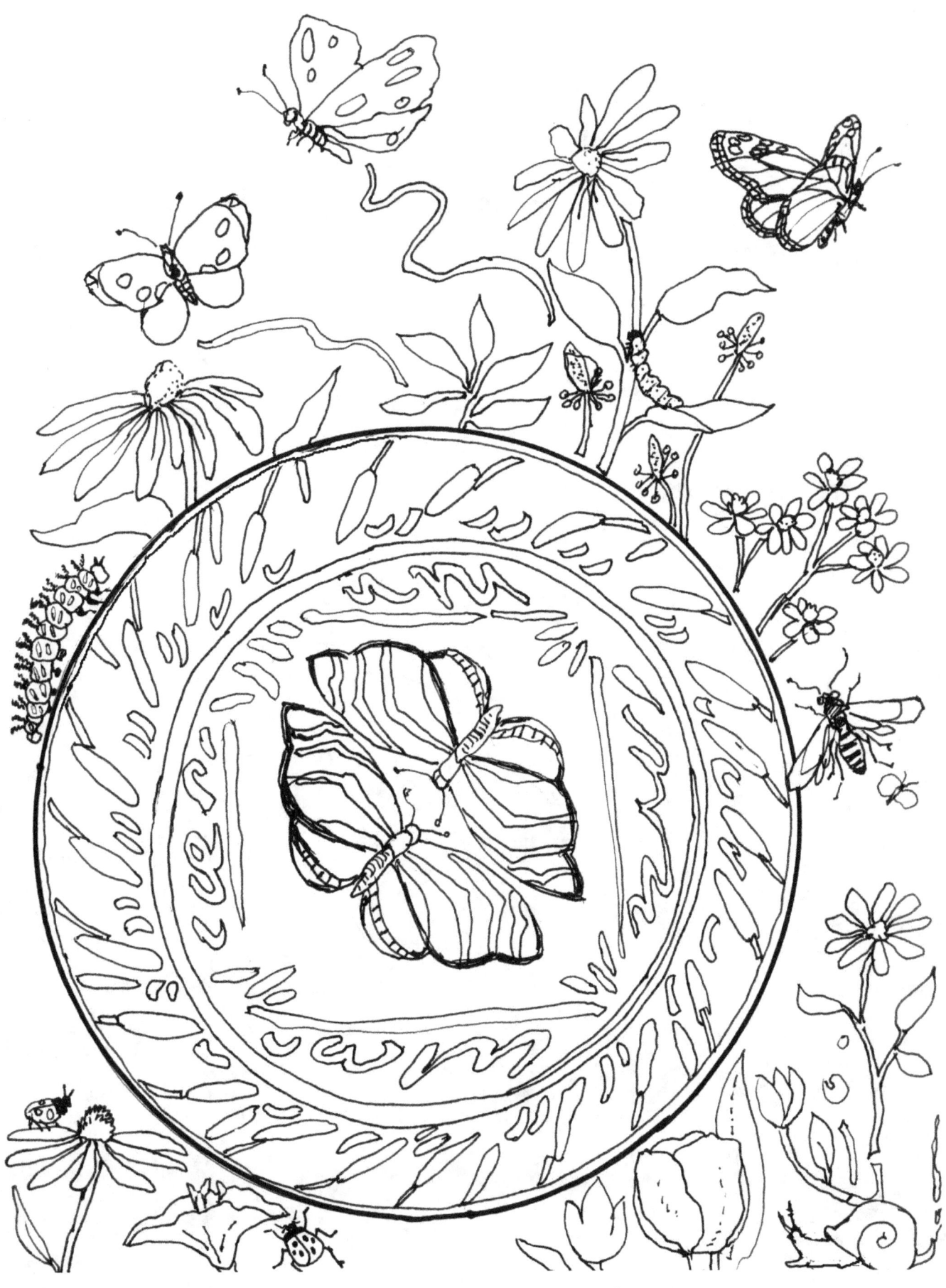

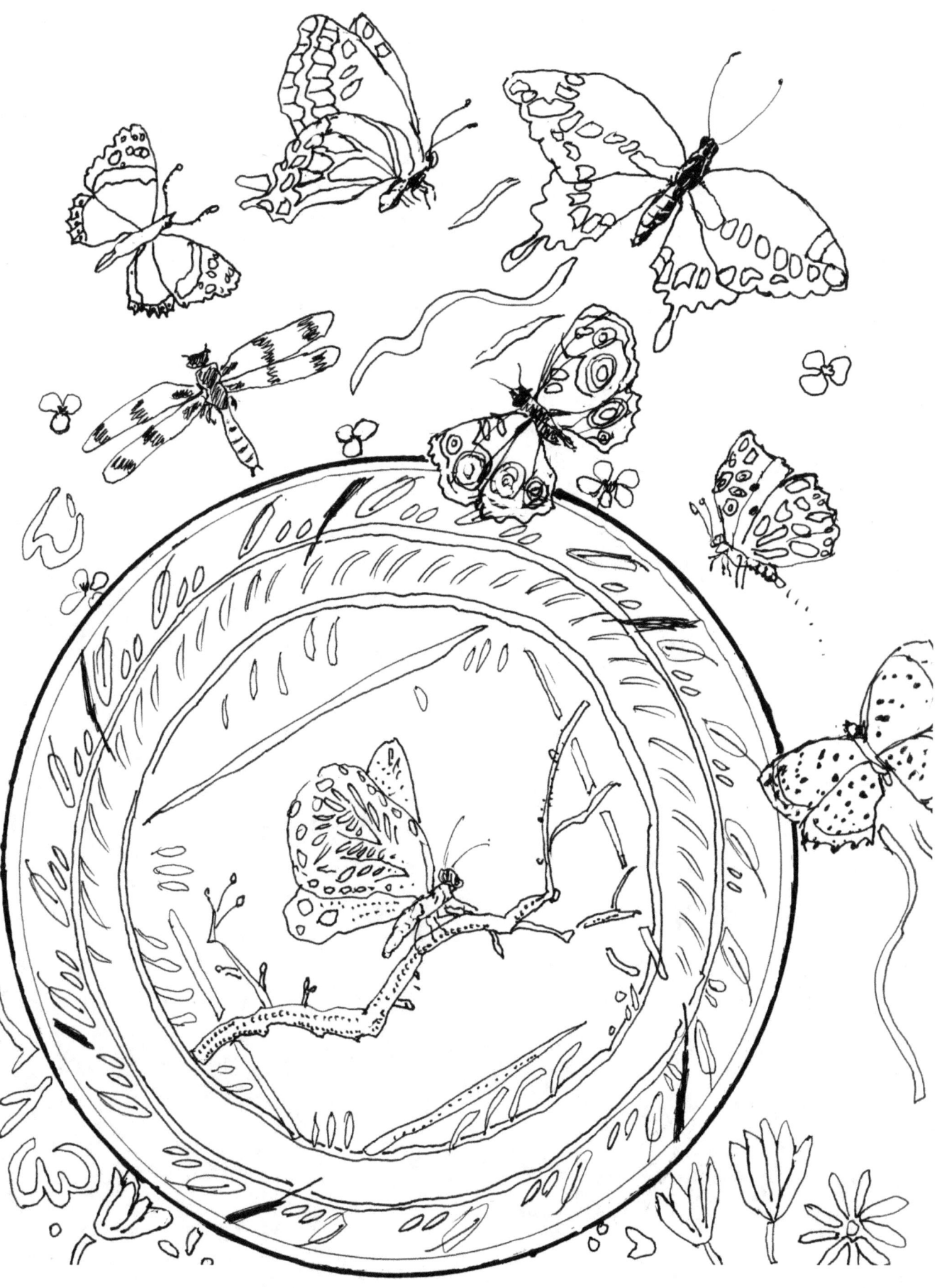

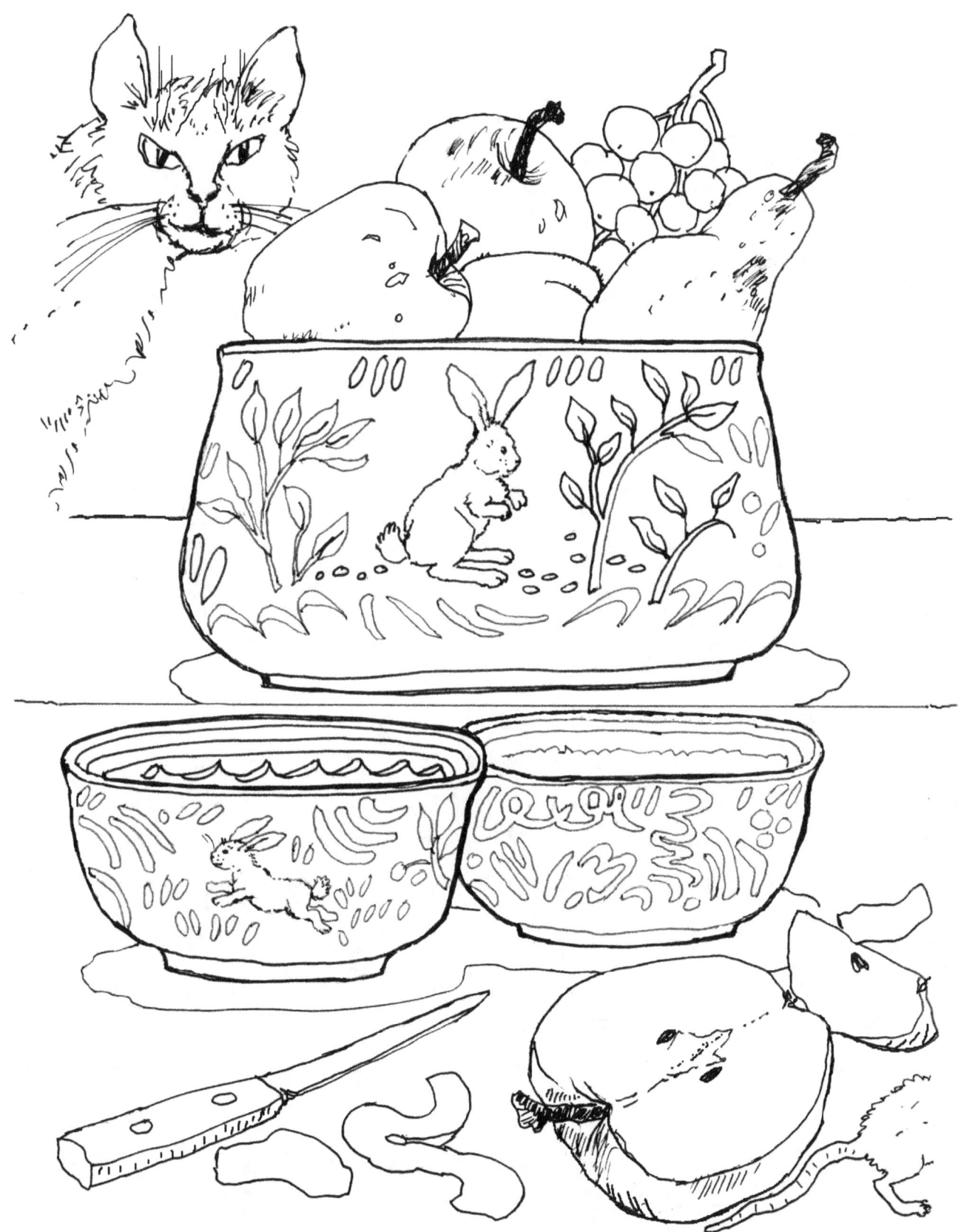

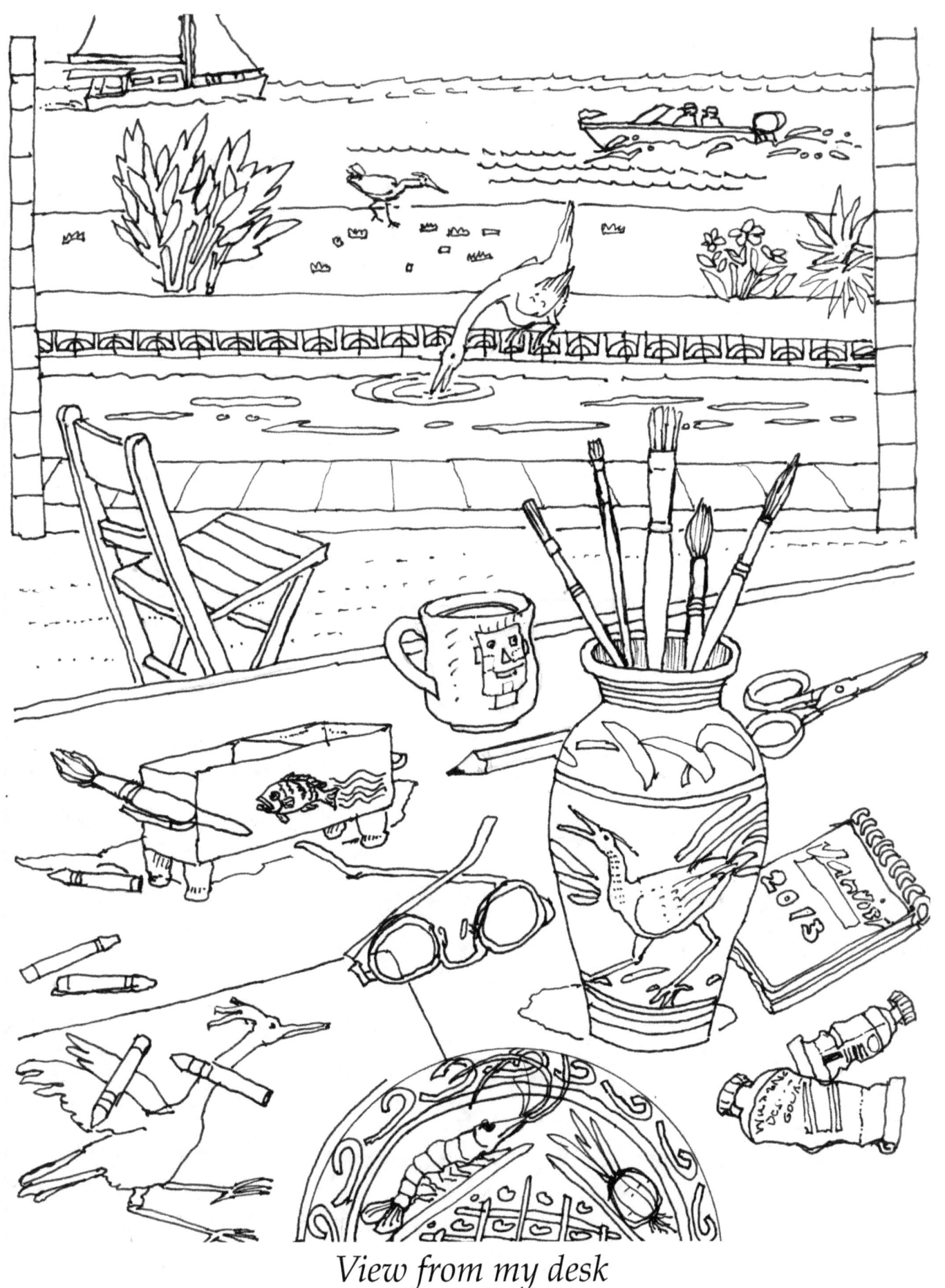

View from my desk

www.ingramcontent.com/pod-product-compliance
Lightning Source LLC
Chambersburg PA
CBHW081620170526
45166CB00009B/3044